RICHARD M. NIXON

RUDY GIULIANI

TWEED

SARAH HOWE

ALEX JONES

WILLIAM P. BARR

JOHN N. MITCHELL

ATCHISON

ALBERT B. FALL

MATT GAETZ

THEODORE BILBO

LINDSEY GRAHAM

J.R. BRINKLEY

ROY M. COHN

RON DE SANTIS

MARJORIE TAYLOR GREENE

CUSTER

WAYNE LAPIERRE

SPIRO T. AGNEW

SIDNEY POWELL

ELISE STEFANIK

ANDREW JACKSON

MICHAEL T. FLYNN

BERNARD MADOFF

NEWT GINGRICH

LEONA HELMSLEY

FORREST

TED CRUZ

MITCH McCONNELL

MIKE LINDELL

MARY MALLON

TILLMAN

A CONFEDERACY OF DUMPTYS

PORTRAITS OF AMERICAN SCOUNDRELS IN VERSE

JOHN LITHGOW

Author of the *NEW YORK TIMES* BESTSELLERS
DUMPTY and *TRUMPTY DUMPTY WANTED A CROWN*

CHRONICLE PRISM

Library of Congress Cataloging-in-Publication Data available.

ISBN 978-1-7972-0947-0

Manufactured in the United States of America.

Illustrations by John Lithgow.
Design by Sara Schneider and Pamela Geismar.
Typesetting by Happenstance Type-O-Rama. Typeset in Adobe Caslon, Brandon Grotesque, and Daft Brush.

10 9 8 7 6 5 4 3 2 1

Chronicle books and gifts are available at special quantity discounts to corporations, professional associations, literacy programs, and other organizations. For details and discount information, please contact our premiums department at corporatesales@chroniclebooks.com or at 1-800-759-0190.

CHRONICLE PRISM

Chronicle Prism is an imprint of Chronicle Books LLC,
680 Second Street, San Francisco, California 94107
www.chronicleprism.com

"When the president does it, that means that it is not illegal."
PRESIDENT RICHARD NIXON, 1977

"We don't pay taxes. Only the little people pay taxes."
LEONA HELMSLEY, 1989

*"The Fraudulent Presidential Election of 2020 will be,
from this day forth, known as THE BIG LIE!"*
DUMPTY, 2021

CONTENTS

Introduction: We've Been Here Before.............................. 7

Prologue: Trumpty Dumpty Was Losing the Race 11

Old Hickory 13

The Man Who Made Kansas Bleed 16

The Wizard of the Saddle.. 20

Nasty Business: The Tale of Boss Tweed.......................... 24

The Great Pyramids of Sarah Howe................................ 29

The Custer Dash.. 33

Centennial Day, 1876 38

The Tale of Typhoid Mary.. 42

The Fall of Fall.. 45

The Goat Gland Doctor 49

Exit Theodore Bilbo 56

The Wonder Boy.. 59

Spiro Zero 64

Happy Fiftieth: A Grand Old Party, Part One................. 68

The Queen of Mean 72

The Secret Life of Newts... 75

Madoff's Trade-Off 78

Happy New Year: A Grand Old Party, Part Two............. 80

A Rogues Gallery 87

Limericks for the Here and Now 88

Dumpty's Dream.. 96

Introduction

WE'VE BEEN HERE BEFORE

For many of you, this book of satirical poems needs no introduction. If you've dipped into my earlier ones, you know what I'm up to. You know my principal targets and my sense of humor, and I'm afraid you will also recognize more than a few of my rhymes.

But for you uninitiated readers, welcome to Dumpty's world.

The other books were my response to the absurdities and occasional horrors of the reign of our forty-fifth president. To me, this man and the bizarre cast of characters in his circle were subjects crying out for satire and mockery. How better to deal with a daily diet of infuriating abuse of power than to make fun of it? Fun is the best possible antidote to ulcerous rage. If I hadn't turned to humor, Dumpty's ruthless and sloppy despotism would have done me in.

For me, this book was a departure. For the most part, I have turned my back on current events. I sat down to write these poems in the weeks following the election of November 3, 2020. Dumpty had been voted out of office. Although he refused to admit defeat (and probably never will), this new collection of poems and drawings was my way of bidding farewell to him and moving on.

I discovered that the best way to move on was to move back in time. I sifted through American history for Dumpty's precursors. I looked for long-forgotten public figures characterized by corruption, bigotry, cowardice, vanity, demagoguery, and, not to put too fine a point on it, stupidity—all those colorful traits that bring Dumpty so quickly to mind.

In prospecting for American scoundrels, I had the good fortune to be married to a historian. My wife, Mary Yeager, an emerita UCLA professor of business history, encouraged my historical approach and steered me toward her colleagues and friends, including professors Stephen Aron, Gary W. Gallagher, Gary Nash, and Joan Waugh.

In addition, I whimsically reached out to notable writers and journalists who make expansive use of historical story-telling in their public commentary. When I asked Doris Kearns Goodwin, Walter Isaacson, Rachel Maddow, and Jon Meacham to suggest subjects for my poems, they responded instantly and enthusiastically, as if I'd invited them to join a lively parlor game.

As my database of villainy grew, an unfolding chronology presented itself and a story began to take shape. Then, halfway through the writing process, Dumpty unleashed his fiery invective at the foot of the Washington Monument and a violent mob assaulted the U.S. Capitol as Congress sat to certify the national election. The chronology had arrived at the present day and my story had its climactic conclusion.

In my view, the Dumpty Era was a grave national trauma, but as I wrote my serio-comic verse, I felt a growing sense of relief in the fact that, as bad as Dumpty was, we've seen worse. He may still be a malign force to be reckoned with, but I'm convinced that no matter how hard he struggles to regain power, Dumpty will eventually drop into the scorned ranks of our history's villains, and we will survive him.

Allow me to offer a few words of acknowledgment.

Three years ago, my impish literary agent, David Kuhn, heard me recite a few of my own rhymes and commanded me to write satirical verse. He steered me to Chronicle Prism and its publisher, Mark Tauber. Since then I have produced three books, working with my canny and delightful editor, Eva Avery, and two endlessly inventive book designers, Pamela Geismar and Sara Schneider. Finally, my assistant, Emma Stack, took care of a hundred details, keeping me from going mad in the grips of meter and rhyme. I am deeply grateful to all of them.

And there's another debt I owe.

When I decided to train my eye on America's nefarious past, the great nineteenth-century political cartoonist Thomas Nast was my inspiration. In fact, I have made him the only subject in this book who is not a scoundrel: he is featured alongside New York City's William "Boss" Tweed in a poem called "Nasty Business" (and this is my chance to point out the pun in its title).

Nast is proof of the power and urgent necessity of satire, in politics and history. Boss Tweed of Tammany Hall was arguably the most corrupt urban powerbroker in any American city ever, but he would probably have drifted from our collective memory if Nast hadn't portrayed him in his devastating cartoons in the pages of *Harper's Weekly*. Tweed has been the image of corruption ever since, but we wouldn't even know what he looked like if it weren't for Thomas Nast. His art is a warning from the grave to all scoundrels in the Dumpty mold. To quote one of my favorite couplets in the book:

You needn't be kindest, or cleanest, or purest,
Just don't ever rankle a caricaturist.

JL, June 15, 2021

TRUMPTY DUMPTY WAS LOSING THE RACE

Trumpty Dumpty was losing the race.
A scowl beclouded his bright orange face.
Watching his margin increasingly widen,
He raged at his nemesis, Sleepy Joe Biden.

The turbulent years of the POTUS's reign
Had shortened his temper and addled his brain.
Like a latter-day Nixon, Capone, or Iago,
He prowled the precincts of plush Mar-a-Lago.

"I WON," he inveighed. "It's a load of FAKE NEWS!
That nitwit's a LOSER, and I NEVER LOSE!"
In a fever, he frantically seized on a plot
To rally his base for a bold coup d'état.

From thence, Dumpty throttled our national life
Over two gruesome months of contention and strife.
Political discourse was drowned in the muck
By the quackery spewed by our manic Lame Duck.

His treachery finally came to fruition:
He stirred up his mob to an act of sedition.
They laid siege (in response to his rash exhortation)
To Biden's electoral certification.

We watched them despoiling the Capitol dome
Like the Visigoths storming the portals of Rome.
"Horrors!" we cried. "He's let anarchy loose!
We've never beheld such despotic abuse!"

But "never," my friends, is an awfully long time.
Our history's replete with corruption and crime.
Scoundrels abound and their damage is ample.
Dumpty is merely the latest example.

And so, for the moment, leave Dumpty aside
And try to take all his offenses in stride.
The voters have finally shown him the door;
We've arrived at a time to revive and restore.
Since we don't have to deal with this swine anymore,
Let's remember the Dumptys who've all gone before.

When Joe Biden was declared the winner of the 2020 U.S. presidential election, President **DONALD J. TRUMP** *claimed the election was "stolen." On January 6, 2021, in a "Save America Rally," Trump delivered an incendiary speech to his followers after which many of them violently assaulted the Capitol. Inside, congressional proceedings were underway to certify the election results.*

OLD HICKORY

Consider Andrew Jackson, the illustrious Old Hickory,
A man of contradictions, of integrity and trickery;
Of prudence and impulsiveness, of cruelty and kindness,
Of coarseness and of dignity, of vision and of blindness.

From his Carolina childhood and his teens in Tennessee,
No one could have guessed the boy's impressive destiny.
Civility and polish? Andy Jackson didn't bother.
He was more a scrappy foundling than a dapper Founding Father.

A trigger-happy recklessness was Jackson's youthful essence,
A temperament that fit a nation's early adolescence.
When southern tribes all mobilized to save their native land,
Andy led an army down to lend a helping hand.

The Choctaw and the Chickasaw, the Cherokee and Creek
Would bow before the havoc that Old Hickory would wreak.
Taking center stage in this chaotic diorama,
He paved the way for statehood in the future Alabama.

Then our embryonic nation, so intemperate and skittish,
Found a unifying hero in the war against the British:
At the Battle of New Orleans, in a stunning blaze of glory,
Andrew Jackson wrote a chapter in our long unfolding story.

His fame begat a résumé that no one could begrudge:
A congressman, a governor, a senator, a judge;
A planter living lavishly and sparing no expense,
Then a member of the pantheon of U.S. presidents.

But once inside the White House, Andy's sterling reputation
Would hit the boiling waters of dispute and condemnation.
Though he boasted a devotion to a country proud and free,
A national disgrace would soon deface his legacy.

This agonizing episode is sadly half-forgotten:
The displacement of a race to clear the South for planting cotton.
With the "Indian problem" missing from the U.S. Constitution,
The Indian Removal Act was Jackson's grim solution.

Abandoning persuasion and resorting to extortion,
He launched a mass migration of near-biblical proportion.
With cruelty unmatched in all these intervening years,
Five tribes were banished westward on the tragic Trail of Tears.

Through the autocratic actions of a suspect national hero,
A proud and ancient multitude was cut to nearly zero.
Behold the bitter consequence of presidential orders:
Ethnic cleansing carried out inside our nation's borders.

Irony will frequently dispense a bitter pill:
Jackson is emblazoned on the twenty-dollar bill.
But the Dumpty years provide the sharpest irony of all:
A portrait of Old Hickory on the Oval Office wall.

In 1830, President **ANDREW JACKSON** *signed the Indian Removal Act. It required the Choctaw, Creek, and Cherokee to relinquish their sovereignty and leave their native lands in the Southeast for new "Indian Territory" west of the Mississippi. Their forced displacement became known as the "Trail of Tears" since thousands of Native Americans died of starvation, exposure, and disease.*

THE MAN WHO MADE KANSAS BLEED

We've been sated with the saga of our bloody Civil War,
But not its dress rehearsal, half a dozen years before.
Of all our fratricidal brawls, the Civil War was worst.
Yet look a little closer: "Bleeding Kansas" happened first.

Mid-century, the nation had to choose its moral fate,
Whether slavery prevailed in every newly minted state.
When Kansas slavers clashed with abolitionist Free Staters,
A Missouri man commanded the Pro-Slaver instigators:

David Rice Atchison, the firebrand of the fray,
Defender of the firm belief that slaves were here to stay.
Atchison's adventures tell a dark and gruesome story—
A bid to export slavery to the Kansas Territory.

As a boyish U.S. senator, he sprung his first surprise,
Legislatively upending the Missouri Compromise.
He intoned his pious mantra, "We should let the voters choose!"
Leaving Kansas abolitionists all shaking in their shoes.

Thus empowered, David hurried home to launch a new offense:
A scheme to people Kansas with like-minded immigrants.
He even formed a namesake town, dispensing sundry favors:
"Join us here in *Atchison*, you sturdy young Pro-Slavers!"

But for David and his followers, the obstacles were legion
Since thousands more Free Staters immigrated to the region.
The quarrel reached a fever pitch in 1855:
An election would determine which arrangement would survive.

But elections can be iffy in a hostile atmosphere,
Especially when held on the American frontier.
Atchison, anticipating loss and dispossession,
Chose violence and voter fraud, coercion and suppression.

He recruited a militia, the Proud Boys of their day.
He called them "Border Ruffians"—Free Staters were their prey.
March thirtieth, Election Day, this bloody-minded throng
Thundered into Kansas in a mob five thousand strong.

They terrorized the countryside and stormed the polling places,
A raid that takes its place among our national disgraces.
The Kansas fields and furrows were soaked with Kansas blood,
And our precious young democracy was trampled in the mud.

The election was contested, leaving chaos in its wake.
The future of the Kansas social contract was at stake:
Two capitals, two governors, two separate societies,
Two state constitutions, and a dueling set of pieties.

Conflicts kept arising like a tide of roiling torrents.
Pro-Slavers staged the sacking of the sleepy town of Lawrence.
Disorder in the Congress shook the nation to its core
With the caning of Charles Sumner on the U.S. Senate floor.

Such eruptions woke the anger of the infamous John Brown.
He led his band of trusties west to bring the slavers down.
Avenging Lawrence, Brown unleashed another killing spree:
Five Pro-Slavers slain beside the Pottawatomie.

These tit-for-tat atrocities and many murders more
Would soon be overshadowed by a cataclysmic war.
But once astute historians send all of their dispatches in,
You'll hear a lot of echoes of Missouri's David Atchison.

And take a moment. Jump ahead 160 years:
Another mob, another siege, more rage and tribal fears.
A young, intemperate senator, defiant, brash, and brawly,
His fist extended in the air: Missourian Josh Hawley.

On Election Day in 1855, Missouri senator **DAVID RICE ATCHISON** *led a militia into the Kansas Territory that stormed polling places and cast fraudulent votes in favor of pro-slavery candidates. These and other violent actions by Atchison were condemned on the floor of the U.S. Senate by* **CHARLES SUMNER**, *who was caned in response by Atchison's pro-slavery allies. These events drew abolitionist* **JOHN BROWN** *to "Bleeding Kansas," where he and his supporters massacred five pro-slavery settlers at Pottawatomie Creek. In 2018, Republican* **JOSH HAWLEY** *was elected U.S. senator from Missouri.*

THE WIZARD OF THE SADDLE

A sore point among southerners
(Perhaps the very sorest)
Is the puzzling dilemma posed
By Nathan Bedford Forrest.

Though in his day they christened him
"The Wizard of the Saddle,"
History has sent him up
Shit's Creek without a paddle.

The offspring of a blacksmith,
Nathan spurned the life plebeian.
He mustered for the Civil War,
The richest Tennessean.

But alas, the source of all his wealth
Was gross commercial knavery:
Cashing in on human souls
By trafficking in slavery.

He rose up through Confederate ranks
As swift as a gazelle,
Dogging even General Grant
And raising holy hell.

He gained his fame on horseback
Where no enemy could sunder him.
At the Battle of Fort Pillow
He had three shot out from under him.

But Fort Pillow also symbolizes
Nathan's darkest stain:
Attempting to surrender,
Three hundred troops were slain.

Three hundred Union soldiers died
With targets on their back,
A tragedy of epic scale
Since most of them were Black.

News about the massacre
Was heard throughout the land,
Since Nathan Bedford Forrest
Was the general in command.

In the South, he was a hero
And the source of injured pride,
But, alas, he was a hero
To the hapless losing side.

When the Ku Klux Klan anointed him
Their very first Grand Wizard,
His reputation sank below
The belly of a lizard.

The legacy achievement
Of a life of raucous ruction
Was the role that Bedford Forrest played
In dooming Reconstruction.

His statues and his monuments
Are disappearing fast,
A stern reminder to us all
That glory doesn't last.

It's echoed in our recent days.
Despite what winning gives us,
Former presidents, take note:
Infamy outlives us.

On April 12, 1864, in the Battle of Fort Pillow in Tennessee, Confederate general **NATHAN BEDFORD FORREST** *and his troops attacked Union forces. During the Union surrender and retreat, Forrest's men massacred more than three hundred Union soldiers, most of them Black. After the war, in 1867, he was elected the first Grand Wizard of the newly formed Ku Klux Klan and served as the group's national leader during the first years of Reconstruction.*

NASTY BUSINESS: THE TALE OF BOSS TWEED

Who can we name that embodies corruption?
A venal volcano that's primed for eruption?
Why, William M. Tweed! Watch him lurch to the stage,
Putting the Guilt in New York's Gilded Age.

Though Tweed was a penniless chair maker's son,
He commanded an empire before he was done.
But a word to the wise for us all to recall:
A lowly cartoonist would trigger his fall.

After trying and failing at every craft,
Young Tweed caught the scent of extortion and graft.
A stint as an ax-wielding fire brigade thug
Infected the lad with the powerbroker bug.

His political clout shot up like a geyser:
Alderman, congressman, town supervisor.
Payoffs and kickbacks were standard routine
As he rose to the top of the New York machine.

This was Tammany Hall, Boss Tweed's private fief,
Ironically named for an Indian chief.
Infested with felons, the law couldn't catch 'em
Once Tammany made him their mighty Grand Sachem.

His strong-arm brutality, cunning, and trickery
Gave him free rein with official hand-pickery:
Peter B. Sweeny, A. Oakey Hall,
Slippery Dick Connolly—and Tweed ran it all.

As the city exploded with commerce and growth,
Tweed defied every statute and broke every oath.
In every transaction, his ring was a player
And taxes were swindled from every taxpayer.

But urban corruption was only the start
Of the brute double-dealing he raised to an art:
With booming new industries high on his docket,
The vast Erie Railroad fit snug in his pocket.

Real estate, too, caught the Boss's keen eye,
A gargantuan slice of the Manhattan pie.
With land confiscated, developed, and sold,
The whole of the Upper East Side turned to gold.

Tweed's crooked career made him richer than Croesus,
A jigsaw of fraud where he owned all the pieces,
A thousand exchanges with Tweed on the take.
The new Brooklyn Bridge? A half ownership stake.

But a criminal empire is destined to tumble.
A quirky reversal would cause it to crumble.
In a sleigh-riding mishap, Tweed's auditor's head
Was crushed by a horse and he ended up dead.

His hasty replacement pored over the books
Revealing a cluster of shysters and crooks.
Armed with the proof of Tweed's manifold crimes,
He ran unafraid to the staid *New York Times*.

NEW YORK, SUNDAY, JULY 29, 1871

We now introduce the aforesaid cartoonist
Who brought down the Boss like a punctured balloonist:
The depictions of Tweed by the great Thomas Nast
Were scathing, satiric, and destined to last.

Nast pictured a slob of Falstaffian bulk,
A baleful, beady-eyed, glowering hulk.
Tweed frantically raged at his impotent goons:
"My people cain't read, *but they see them cartoons!*"

Nast and the *Times* spelled the end of Boss Tweed,
An epic collapse from the wages of greed.
Jailed on all charges, he fought them in vain.
He even escaped once and bolted for Spain.

But back in Manhattan, bereft of his fame,
Tweed languished in lockup and wallowed in shame.
Of his Gilded Age pelf there remained not a trace.
At the Ludlow Street Prison, he died in disgrace.

So what do we learn from Tweed's gloomy demise?
What prudent perception to open our eyes?
A lesson to teach both defendant and jurist,
From youngest beginner right up to maturest:
You needn't be kindest, or cleanest, or purest,
Just don't ever rankle a caricaturist.

New York City political boss **WILLIAM M. TWEED** *stole as much as forty-five million dollars from New York taxpayers in the 1860s and '70s. His ring, which controlled the city's finances, included Mayor* **A. OAKEY HALL**, *City Chamberlain and Park Commissioner* **PETER B. SWEENY**, *and Comptroller* **RICHARD B. "SLIPPERY DICK" CONNOLLY**. *After the* New York Times *exposed his gigantic fraud in 1871, Tweed was ultimately convicted on 204 counts and died in prison.*

THE GREAT PYRAMIDS OF SARAH HOWE

The masculine cast of this villainous crowd
Makes it seem like a club with no women allowed.
The cigar, the spittoon, the brandy and snifter
Are the props of the stereotypical grifter.

But into our den of American thieves
Steps a female with multiple tricks up her sleeves.
She offers a curtsy instead of a bow:
A bona fide scoundrel, petite Sarah Howe.

A Boston-bred waif who was born to privation,
Sarah embarked on a life of predation.
In the opéra bouffe of our grand Gilded Age,
She escaped from the pit and climbed onto the stage.

Of her earlier history there's barely a word:
She discarded two husbands and buried a third.
But then as a widow, she started to traffic
In schemes that exploited her own demographic.

These women bought everything Sarah was selling
Through astral projections and fake fortune-telling.
But a scam that eluded their closer attention
Made Sarah the mother of venal invention.

Her targets gave off the aroma of gold:
Gullible, wealthy, and most of them old.
So rummaging through her chicanery closet,
She fashioned a company called Ladies' Deposit.

Eight percent interest was instantly paid
On deposits from each unsuspecting old maid.
Within weeks Sarah reaped a gargantuan sum
Secured by prospective deposits to come.

Sly as a cat that has stolen the cream,
She'd hit on a hoary old pyramid scheme.
But she figured her marks would be different from males:
Secretive spinsters would never tell tales.

But Sarah fell prey to her own arrant greed.
Her business was growing too big to succeed.
A nosy reporter in full spinster drag
Sneaked into her office and raised a red flag.

News of her stratagem spread through the nation,
Her victims were fraught with their victimization.
Rage and misogyny triggered her fall:
Down came the pyramid, Sarah and all.

The judge and the jury (exclusively male)
Sentenced poor Sarah to three years in jail.
But once she completed her time in the tank,
She was at it again, with the Women's Bank.

Another quick bundle, another quick bust,
Another cruel breach of a sisterhood's trust,
Another explosion of public excitement,
But this time she vanished before her indictment.

In town after town she would set up her trade;
For Chicago she launched Ladies Provident Aid.
Over and over, her schemes came to naught,
And returning to Boston, at last she was caught.

Caught and released! Sarah's legend enlarges:
None of her ladies would bring any charges.
After all of the scandal and strife that befell her,
She ended her tour as a poor fortune-teller.

A women's crusader ahead of her time,
Sarah broke the glass ceiling of white-collar crime.
So give her some credit! Let's hear a few cheers!
She beat Carlo Ponzi by forty-one years!

SARAH HOWE, *a Boston fortune-teller, made her own fortune in 1879 and 1880 using a pyramid scheme that was later associated with* **CARLO PONZI**. *She served three years in prison for fraud, but then reprised her scheme in other cities. After another arrest in 1888, she resumed her previous career of fortune-telling.*

THE CUSTER DASH

Of all of the scoundrels presented herewith,
One man was a genius at forging his myth.
Bathed in the limelight of counterfeit luster,
Behold the Boy General, George Armstrong Custer!

Yes, Custer, that sterling American brand,
The eponymous martyr of Custer's Last Stand,
Was a cat of a different historical stripe
Whose story was born of vainglory and hype.

Delinquent at West Point and last in his class,
Through charm and connivance, he managed to pass.
Brash and unbridled, his future was bleak
'Til Fort Sumter ignited his long lucky streak.

Making good use of the grim Civil War,
Custer shot up through the raw Union corps.
A brigadier general at age twenty-three,
He fixed his attention on posterity.

With his reckless heroics and brazen grandstanding,
The arc of his story was swiftly expanding.
He penned his own press with theatrical flash,
Touting "Custer's Luck" and "The Custer Dash."

He looked upon war as performative art
And costumed himself to embody his part,
With sombreros and epaulets, tassels to spare,
And cinnamon scenting his flowing blond hair.

His thespian vanity had to be fed
Even in front of the troops that he led.
Tilting with death as a spectator sport,
The cavalry charge was his fustian forte.

Custer's theatrics, of course, came in handy:
His Gettysburg turn was a stiff shot of brandy.
The rout of Jeb Stuart was told near and far
And George Armstrong Custer emerged as a *star*!

The South had surrendered. The Union had won.
But Custer still clung to his saber and gun.
With the thrill of the chase in his veins and his pores,
He pointed his horse to the Indian Wars.

The nation was opening broad new expanses,
Spreading throughout Oklahoma and Kansas.
But the Pawnee, Arapaho, Sioux, and Cheyenne
Were resisting America's grand master plan.

Custer in buckskin cried, "Leave it to me!
I'm all for expanding the Land of the Free!
My army and I will take matters in hand!
We'll break all their treaties and take all their land!"

An unlikely companion rode out by his side,
Elizabeth Bacon, his Civil War bride.
Libbie played a dual role in their marital pact,
A wife and a press agent, hawking his act.

Custer, the reckless and rash martinet,
Needed all the good press he could possibly get.
His intemperance, peppered with blunt self-promotion,
Brought censure, court-martial, reproach, and demotion.

Libbie stepped in as his image adjuster,
Demanding the public let Custer be Custer.
She used every arrow she had in her quiver
To soften the carnage at Washita River.

But the real Custer legend was finally born
On the Montana plains by the Little Bighorn.
When Crazy Horse and his warriors struck,
They rang down the curtain on Custer's Luck.

Custer's finale was self-orchestrated,
His cavalry trapped and annihilated.
He died an impetuous, foolhardy jerk,
But Libbie recovered and went right to work.

She gilded his story and burnished his name,
A fastidious keeper of Custer's flame.
Over fifty-six years of devout adulation,
She saved him from factual deconsecration.

Most of us swallowed her rapt hagiography,
Suckers for drama and martial pornography.
We shucked our misgivings and struck up the band
For the spurious fable of Custer's Last Stand.

But today, Custer's epic has grown cautionary,
A timely reminder to warn the unwary:
When a scoundrel from history exits the stage,
Fictions will turn into facts as they age.

After service in the Civil War—including the Union victory at Gettysburg over Confederate general **JEB STUART**—*cavalry commander* **GEORGE ARMSTRONG CUSTER** *went on to fight in the Indian Wars as a lieutenant colonel. In 1876, he was killed at the Battle of Little Bighorn. His wife,* **ELIZABETH BACON**, *continued to promote his public image with speeches and books about him.*

CENTENNIAL DAY, 1876

They say with Appomattox, the Confederacy was done—
After Gettysburg and Shiloh, Antietam and Bull Run.
But with all the deep divisions that our history has wrought,
Examples prove the Civil War continues to be fought.

Take a brief excursion through historical arcana,
Starting off with Colfax, in mid-Louisiana;
Add Tulsa, Slocum, Wilmington, Polk County, Thibodaux,
And a dozen other massacres from not so long ago.

Centennial Day in Hamburg! The birthday of the nation!
A crush of South Carolinians whooped in celebration.
A snappy Black militia headed up a joyful crowd:
Emancipated Freedmen, parading tall and proud.

But a national election loomed, a few short months away.
Local ex-Confederates foresaw Redemption Day.
With the Civil War behind them, their intent was crystal clear:
Restore their former glory through ferocity and fear.

They called themselves the Red Shirts, a fire-breathing scourge,
Pouring into Hamburg to terrorize and purge.
Benjamin Ryan Tillman was the leader of this brood,
A plantation owner fixed on reinstating servitude.

A thousand strong, the Red Shirt throng beset the Black gendarmerie
Then chased them from the safety and protection of their armory.
Eight killed and dozens wounded by the time their rage was sated;
Among the dead the local marshal, slain and mutilated.

Though ninety were indicted for this lawless insurrection,
Their trials were postponed until the pending postelection—
But the ringing voice of justice in the end was sadly muted:
Of all the bloody Red Shirts, not a one was prosecuted.

As for Tillman, he took mutiny and murder in his stride,
Flaunting Hamburg carnage as a point of racial pride.
In politics the vilest, most bigoted of men,
As a governor and senator, they called him "Pitchfork Ben."

But Hamburg was the preview to an existential fix:
The contested presidential race of 1876.
The South had risen once again to even up the score,
Wielding politics and terror to refight the Civil War.

For them the ballot deadlock, with its bitter tribal rift,
Turned out to be an unexpected hundredth birthday gift.
They scuttled Reconstruction with their faces all aglow:
"You can have your president if we can have Jim Crow!"

The massacre in Hamburg dealt a tragic mortal wound,
Its dwindling population rendered broken and marooned;
1927 saw its poignant dying day:
The Savannah River overflowed and washed the town away.

Today a golf course spreads across the broad and breezy land
Where the peaceable community of Hamburg used to stand.
As Carolina golfers walk the fairways and the greens,
The thought of strife and slaughter almost never intervenes.

But take a moment. Think about the sixth of January,
A blast of passion, murderous and insurrectionary.
Then picture Trumpty Dumpty, the man who would be king,
Standing on the tee box and practicing his swing.

In 1876, **BENJAMIN RYAN TILLMAN** *led a white paramilitary group, called the Red Shirts, that massacred Black militiamen in the town of Hamburg, South Carolina, and used violence to suppress Black votes. Tillman was elected governor of South Carolina in 1890 and became a U.S. senator four years later. During his twenty-three years in the Senate, he supported white supremacy, lynching, and the use of anti-Black terror to win elections.*

THE TALE OF TYPHOID MARY

The tale of Typhoid Mary
In New York of yesteryear
Tells us justice can miscarry
And that guilt is seldom clear.

Mary Mallon was an Irish cook
A hundred years ago.
She carried typhus in her veins,
But Mary didn't know.

She fed a wealthy household once
In tony Oyster Bay.
Half the family fell ill
But Mary slipped away.

George Soper, sanitation sleuth
Invited to the scene,
Suspected Mary Mallon,
Who was nowhere to be seen.

Soper sifted through her past
From many years ago:
Everywhere that Mary went,
The scourge was sure to go.

He took the role of Sherlock Holmes
And gathered every clue,
Tracking Mary down at last
On swank Park Avenue.

Another stove, another sink,
Another family stricken.
Soper in the entry hall:
The plot began to thicken.

When Soper started in to state
The facts from heretofore,
Brawny Mary took a knife
And chased him out the door.

She then began a frantic game,
Hygienic cat and mouse:
Contaminating dozens
As she stole from house to house.

The press took note of Soper
And his Irish adversary.
From thence Miss Mallon, to her shame,
Was branded "Typhoid Mary."

She took the name of Mary Brown
And cooked in secrecy,
Infecting scores of others
At the Sloane infirmary.

Soper collared her at last,
His triumphant final scene,
And Mary's final years were spent
In lonely quarantine.

A villainess or heroine?
Opprobrium or praise?
The tale of Typhoid Mary
And the curse she had to carry
Is aptly cautionary
In our own pandemic days.

MARY MALLON *was an asymptomatic carrier of typhoid from her birth in 1869. She worked as a cook for New York families, and when many people she fed became sick, investigator* **GEORGE SOPER** *traced the outbreaks to her. Dubbed "Typhoid Mary," Mallon died after nearly three decades in forced quarantine.*

THE FALL OF FALL

His name and his infamy few will recall.
We've all but forgotten the late Albert Fall.
But a hundred years later, his story hits home:
The scandalous tale of the Teapot Dome.

A cotton mill urchin, asthmatic but plucky,
Fall bolted from hardscrabble Frankfort, Kentucky.
Rousting about 'til his seventeenth year,
He at last came to rest on the Southwest frontier.

He began as a teacher while teaching himself.
Contracts and codicils cluttered his shelf.
As a circuit attorney, he rolled up his sleeves,
Defender of murderers, rustlers, and thieves.

Though he rose to be councilman, judge, and AG,
Nothing came near what he wanted to be.
But with statehood, New Mexico paid him a call:
Fortune and favor befell Albert Fall.

He was fingered for senator! Fall's greatest feat!
And in less than a decade a Cabinet seat!
Interior was entrusted to Albert's safeguarding,
Installed by the cronies of Warren G. Harding.

They were dubbed the Ohio Gang. Timorous Fall
Was held in their shady political thrall,
While Harding, the putative head of the land,
Meekly reclined in the palm of their hand.

Politicians and fat cats in equal proportion,
The Gang were past masters at theft and extortion.
From the moment that Albert took over his seat,
They taught him to swindle, finagle, and cheat.

Among them, a notably devious pair
Were Edward Doheny and Harry Sinclair.
The two were illicitly out for a killing
In licensing oil exploration and drilling.

With Fall as their pawn, they were able to choose
Which bidders would win and which bidders would lose.
They kept for themselves the most lucrative prize
In Wyoming, the state where the Teapot Dome lies.

With Albert in league with this covetous cult
Political scandal was bound to result.
When at last the extent of his graft was unveiled,
He was driven from office, convicted, and jailed.

Thus Albert was pounded by justice's fist.
Sinclair and Doheny? A slap on the wrist.
As for Harding, that feckless, libidinous lout,
Dead in office before all the garbage spilled out.

Such was the fall of poor Albert Fall
Of the Teapot connivers, the saddest of all.
He ended his days in privation and shame.
Small wonder so few will remember his name.

There's a moral, of course, to this pitiful fable
Of civil depravity, under the table:
Though lessons are legion as history churns,
A grifter with gifts to bestow never learns.

In 1921, President **WARREN G. HARDING** *appointed New Mexico Senator* **ALBERT FALL** *as secretary of the interior. After accepting bribes, Fall awarded oilmen* **EDWARD DOHENY** *and* **HARRY SINCLAIR** *leases to drill in U.S. Naval Reserves in Elk Hills, California, and the Teapot Dome Field in Wyoming. Fall was convicted of bribery and conspiracy in 1929 and jailed, the first former cabinet member to be convicted of a crime.*

THE GOAT GLAND DOCTOR

Of all these rogues, one stands apart.
His turpitude is off the chart.
Our other crooks are downright twinkly
Next to Dr. John R. Brinkley.

The twentieth century's early years
Saw war, disease, mistrust, and tears.
When panic, dread, and angst abound,
John Brinkley's ilk finds fertile ground.

A child of Appalachian dearth,
The boy bamboozled from his birth.
His knack for fiction, fraud, and flackery
Prefigured Brinkley's rampant quackery.

Armed with snake oil, ointments, pills,
And scrip from fake diploma mills,
He hawked "a cure for all your woes"
At county fairs and medicine shows.

This hectic work was not much fun:
Flimflam kept him on the run.
Like all corrupt commercial predators,
John was dogged by cops and creditors.

A wife named Minnie eased his strife,
But John had grown to hate his life.
He paused at last and, taking stock,
Became a small-town family doc.

He and Minnie took their chances,
Settling down in Milford, Kansas.
Hayseed jayhawks, tanned and wrinkly,
Welcomed Dr. John R. Brinkley.

In his office, one spring morn,
John's exalted brand was born:
A farmer, shedding all civility,
Bemoaned the loss of his virility.

Dr. Brinkley, thinking fast,
Riffled through his bogus past.
"I know what to do!" he cried,
And lugged a neighbor's goat inside.

Soon the farmer burst with joy:
His wife produced a baby boy!
Reporters rushed to amply quote him:
"Doc sewed goat gland in m'scrotum!"

The novel Brinkley operation
Caused a Milford-wide sensation.
Locals clamored for his service,
Though their goats were plainly nervous.

Goat gland treatments were extolled
Well beyond the Milford fold.
Wanting all the world to know,
Brinkley turned to radio.

The medium, in its infancy,
Had found an ardent devotee:
Dr. Brinkley, talk-show star,
Peddled goat gland near and far.

Country music! Homey chatter!
Goat gland for your bowels and bladder!
Set your dial: KFKB!
A radio station, just for me!

John appeared to have it all,
But vexing signs foretold his fall.
Medical rules and media regs
Stole the goose's golden eggs.

Morris Fishbein, Brinkley hater,
AMA's investigator,
Dragooned the Kansas Medical Board
To put John's practice to the sword.

To Brinkley this was just a blip:
He sought the Kansas governorship.
But once they took his station too,
He told the state that he was through.

John and Minnie motored down
And found a Texas border town:
Del Rio, on the Rio Grande,
Where Brinkley took his final stand.

His lavish clinic made a splash,
Built with stacks of Kansas cash.
Every day it topped its quota,
Lured by Brinkley's hircine scrota.

Across the river: Mexico!
Where John returned to radio.
Free from U.S. regulation,
He pitched his wares across the nation.

This was Brinkley's golden age,
A pundit on the national stage.
Among the nostrums he dispersed?
Hitler. And "America First."

His Texas home was Xanadu:
A mansion, with a private zoo.
But all his yachts and Cadillacs
Hid a spiderweb of cracks.

Alas, his salad days were fleeting.
Fishbein's drum was grimly beating.
Out came all the damning facts
Of Brinkley's goat-related acts.

Tax fraud, mail fraud, needless death,
Crimes to take away your breath;
Slander, suits, and bankruptcies
Brought John Brinkley to his knees.

His fortune gone, his honor stained,
A gruesome end was foreordained.
Toppled from his lofty throne,
The Goat Gland Doctor died alone.

Today, John Brinkley's name denotes
Grifters, gulls, and glands of goats.
Despite his brief celebrity,
There's nothing left but mockery.
Recall his sorry legacy
When pondering what your own might be.

DR. JOHN ROMULUS BRINKLEY *made millions by implanting goat gonads into men's testicles and women's abdomens, claiming the process would boost virility and fertility and cure a wide range of ailments. After he was exposed by medical investigator* **MORRIS FISHBEIN**, *he declared bankruptcy in 1941 and died in poverty a year later.*

EXIT THEODORE BILBO

Theodore Bilbo, bulwark
Of the Anglo-Saxon race,
Gave ignorance and zealotry
A pink, reptilian face.

Cracker-barrel populism,
Bred in the Depression,
Found in Teddy Bilbo
Its ultimate expression.

A Mississippi senator
(And governor at that),
Bilbo was the quintessential
Racist Dixiecrat.

At five foot two, a feverish
And hyperactive stoat,
If Ted had ever got his way,
Black folks would never vote.

Advancing white supremacy
He fought with tooth and claw,
Stridently opposing
Every anti-lynching law.

And demented by a phobic fear
Of rife miscegenation,
Bilbo fiercely advocated
Black repatriation.

With all the bile and bigotry
A senator could muster,
He gave new life to old Jim Crow
Through endless filibuster.

A logorrheic windbag,
The worst in all the South,
His grim, ironic cause of death
Was cancer of the mouth.

When Teddy Bilbo passed away,
His nurses all contrived
To leave him in his bed until
Frank Wilderson arrived.

Frank, a young Black orderly,
Was told to clean and clear him.
"If Teddy was alive," said he,
"He'd never let me near him."

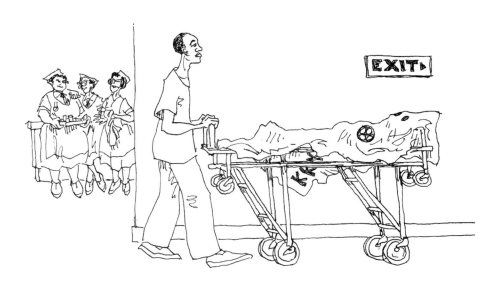

Few remember Teddy Bilbo
As the decades rumble by.
But cruelty and hatred
Sadly never seem to die.

THEODORE BILBO *served twice as governor of Mississippi and, from 1935 to 1947, represented the state in the U.S. Senate. A member of the Ku Klux Klan, he fought to repatriate Black citizens to Africa as a solution to unemployment during the Great Depression. When he died at the Ochsner Clinic in New Orleans, his body was removed by* **FRANK WILDERSON,** *a Black student at Xavier University who worked as an orderly. Wilderson later served as vice president of the University of Minnesota.*

THE WONDER BOY

Ask any ten New Yorkers. All the older ones will know
The story of a human snake from fifty years ago.
They'll tell the tale of Roy M. Cohn, an avatar of spite,
With curling lip, dyspeptic eye, and venom in his bite.

An only child descended from a rich dynastic clan,
Roy was smothered by his mother from the day his life began.
He graduated law school at the tender age of twenty,
A Wonder Boy adopted by the Gotham cognoscenti.

The Rosenbergs were standing trial and facing execution.
The Wonder Boy was sent to court to boost the prosecution.
He screamed for their conviction with his every gasping breath
And made his name when both of them were cruelly put to death.

Watching Roy pursue the case with such ferocious glee,
J. Edgar Hoover plucked him up and brought him to DC.
All through Hoover's anti-communistic reign of fear,
Roy M. Cohn the Wonder Boy had Joe McCarthy's ear.

A pair of dime-store villains both malevolent and smarmy,
Roy was there for Joe's pursuit of commies in the Army.
It marked McCarthy's downfall, with another story line:
Roy's infatuation with co-counsel David Schine.

For Roy was gay, a simple fact that everybody posited,
Yet all his life, the Wonder Boy was obstinately closeted.
He even led a fierce campaign of staggering hypocrisy,
Terrorizing gays throughout the federal bureaucracy.

When Joe McCarthy's power in DC began to slip,
Roy scampered like a frisky rat from off a sinking ship.
Returning to Manhattan, he began a new career:
Perverting justice, spreading lies, and propagating fear.

The '60s in the city were a dark and dirty time.
Every tabloid headline shrieked of scandal, sin, and crime.
Like a pig in shit, the Wonder Boy delighted in his job
And became the go-to lawyer for the New York City mob.

His circle was a carousel of thugs and glitterati:
Andy Warhol, Norman Mailer, Barbara Walters, and John Gotti.
He prowled the city courtrooms like a mugger with a knife,
But in Upper East Side luxe, he led a lurid double life.

Enter youthful Dumpty in a legal spot of bother:
A bias charge directed at his mobbed-up builder father.
They hired Roy, who got them off without a guilty plea,
And thus was forged an ironclad bond in perpetuity.

Roy took Dumpty by the hand, an eager protégé,
And schooled him in a crooked maxim: *Crime will often pay*.
"Admit to nothing!" Roy exclaimed. "The truth was meant for spinning!
Your mantra every waking hour is *Winning! Winning! Winning!*"

The fruits of Dumpty's tutelage will not escape your notice:
A thirty-year ascent that elevated him to POTUS.
In his every smear and libel, every strategy and ploy,
You can spot the rotten influence of Roy the Wonder Boy.

In his later years, the Wonder Boy would push his luck too far.
His legal misdemeanors got him booted from the bar.
A snake who's lost his poison is a dog who's had his day:
His ritzy crowd of glitzy friends began to turn away.

Roy's story ended poignantly, an AIDS-related death,
A disease he disavowed until his final dying breath.
His legend was forgotten but was parroted anew
When his spirit re-emerged on Pennsylvania Avenue.

For with Dumpty in the White House, Roy's amoral education
Provided guiding principles for governing the nation.
Pacing after midnight, in his quarters all alone,
Dumpty howled in desperation:

"WHERE IS MY ROY COHN?!"

In 1951, **ROY M. COHN,** *a young assistant U.S. attorney in Manhattan, prosecuted and argued for the execution of* **JULIUS AND ETHEL ROSENBERG**—*American citizens convicted of spying for the Soviet Union. FBI Director* **J. EDGAR HOOVER** *recommended him for the job of chief counsel for Senator* **JOSEPH MCCARTHY.** *Cohn and his assistant* **DAVID SCHINE** *were McCarthy's hatchet men as he aggressively targeted suspected communists and homosexuals. After the Senate condemned McCarthy in 1954, Cohn established a legal practice in Manhattan. In 1986, he was disbarred for unethical conduct, and soon after, he died of AIDS.*

SPIRO ZERO

Any list of miscreants is certain to include
Spiro Agnew, the embodiment of venal turpitude.
His history of larceny began in Baltimore,
With penny-ante bribery behind an office door.

Spiro was unburdened by a civic sense of guilt.
He took a piece of everything the County Council built.
After pocketing a cut of every rebar, brick, and stanchion,
He took up residence inside the stately governor's mansion.

As chief exec of Maryland, he upped his dirty game,
Then as Richard Nixon's running mate, we got to know his name.
The role of Dick's attack dog suited Spiro to a T
And we ended up electing a felonious VP.

For years the dollars mounted up, surpassing all his hopes,
Delivered to the White House stuffed in bulging envelopes.
Like a fat and happy porker, Spiro Agnew was in clover,
Unaware his sunny skies would soon be clouding over.

Meanwhile, back in Baltimore, three legal eager beavers
Caught a whiff of underhanded givers and receivers.
The three uncovered graft that would have shocked the likes of Nero
And a trail of solid evidence that led them straight to Spiro.

Full of dread, the threesome sped to Washington, DC,
And face-to-face they made their case to Nixon's prim AG.
This was Elliot Richardson, bespectacled patrician,
A gentleman embarked upon an even darker mission.

The House was holding hearings weighing criminal intent:
"Obstructing justice" charged against the sitting president.
The Baltimore attorneys thus were piling Elliot's plate
With an extra load of trouble in the midst of *WATERGATE!*

The AG's brain exploded at the news of Spiro's graft,
Criminal behavior taxing all his legal craft.
A disaster lay before him like a chasm wide and deep:
The concurrent prosecution of a POTUS and a veep.

The removal of the president could happen any time,
Making way for Spiro, a leviathan of crime.
Elliot saw the task at hand, the clock was ticking down:
Get him out of office quick and kick him out of town!

With a leak, the press descended. Like a weed, the scandal grew.
For a moment, even Watergate was banished to page two.
Spiro's fiery countercharge defied his certain fate,
Excoriating Fake News and denouncing the Deep State.

But faced with facts too incontestable to fight,
He struck a deal with Elliot to vanish in the night.
No prison term, no recompense, his felonies ignored,
His punishment: a soul disgraced, replaced by Gerald Ford.

So Elliot had pulled it off, with subtlety and flair.
But he wasn't quite so lucky with the Watergate affair.
The Saturday Night Massacre was ten short days away:
Richardson was ousted when he'd just rejoined the fray.

When Spiro Agnew walked away, the public shed no tears.
He languished in obscurity for twenty-three more years.
He wrote a pair of worthless books, but no one ever read them.
If there were words of praise for Spiro, no one ever said them.

His rise and fall can teach us all a tarnished golden rule:
The higher the heights from which you drop, the more you look the fool.
He lived a life of vice, and yet a broken system let him.
The kindest homage we can pay is simply to forget him.

In 1973, President **RICHARD M. NIXON'S** *vice president*
SPIRO AGNEW *was investigated for criminal conspiracy,
bribery, extortion, and tax fraud. He later resigned and pleaded
no contest to tax evasion after negotiating an agreement with
Attorney General* **ELLIOT RICHARDSON** *that spared him
jail time. Nixon replaced Agnew with* **GERALD FORD**. *Six
months later, Nixon resigned from office as a result of the Watergate
scandal.*

HAPPY FIFTIETH
A GRAND OLD PARTY, PART ONE

Gather round, beloved chums!
All you Watergate alums!
An anniversary impends
For Tricky Dick's devoted friends.
Half a century is behind you
Since the scandal that defined you.
Time to reminisce and party,
Raise a toast sincere and hearty,
Spray on all your cheap perfumes:
Your fiftieth reunion looms!

The band performs a fanfare which'll
Welcome John and Martha Mitchell.
Sizing up the groaning board
Are E. Howard Hunt and James McCord,
And flushed with bubbly, gay and giddy,
Who'd have thought? G. Gordon Liddy!
There's the saturnine Chuck Colson,
Sipping on a lukewarm Molson,
With Dwight Chapin, dark and dour,
On his second whiskey sour.
The chocolate fountain overwhelms
Chocoholic Richard Helms,
And check out hangdog Robert Mardian,
Looking like he's lost his guardian.
Beside him sits Rose Mary Woods,
The femme fatale who's got the goods.
And there's that lackey Jeb Magruder,
Skulking like a glum intruder,

Hit with fistfuls of confetti
Thrown by impish Don Segretti.
John Ehrlichman, that brutish lout,
Displays his omnipresent pout.
And giving up on having fun,
Is stoic H. R. Haldeman
Who grimly growls, "Et tu Brute,"
As John Dean eyes a canapé.

When at last the party ends,
The crowd remembers absent friends.
Someone makes a drunken toast
To Richard Nixon's ghoulish ghost.
"Thank you, Dick!" the wag proclaims,
"For besmirching all our names!
Thanks for poisoning our story,
For fifty years in purgatory,
For all the torment and travail,
And sending all of us to jail.
Tonight we curse our sorry fate:
Thanks a lot for Watergate!"

Dozens of members of the administration of President **RICHARD NIXON** *were caught up in the Watergate scandal resulting from the "third-rate burglary" of Democratic Party headquarters in the Watergate Hotel. Among them were the following:*

JOHN MITCHELL, *Nixon's former attorney general and head of the Committee for the Re-election of the President, known as CREEP (nineteen months in federal prison)*

MARTHA MITCHELL, *nicknamed "Martha the Mouth," who was married to John Mitchell*

E. HOWARD HUNT, *a former intelligence officer and Watergate burglar (thirty-three months in federal prison)*

JAMES MCCORD, *a former CIA officer and Watergate burglar (four months in federal prison)*

G. GORDON LIDDY, *an attorney, former FBI agent, and Watergate conspirator (fifty-two months in federal prison)*

CHUCK COLSON, *attorney and special counsel to President Nixon (seven months in federal prison)*

DWIGHT CHAPIN, *deputy assistant to President Nixon (nine months in federal prison)*

RICHARD HELMS, *director of the CIA from 1966 to 1973*

ROBERT MARDIAN, *a political coordinator for CREEP*

ROSE MARY WOODS, *Nixon's secretary*

JEB MAGRUDER, *deputy director of CREEP (seven months in federal prison)*

DONALD SEGRETTI, *who ran the dirty tricks campaign against the Democrats for CREEP (four and a half months in federal prison)*

JOHN EHRLICHMAN, *counsel and assistant to the president for domestic affairs (eighteen months in federal prison)*

H. R. HALDEMAN, *Nixon's chief of staff, who was convicted of conspiracy and obstruction of justice (eighteen months in federal prison)*

JOHN DEAN, *Nixon's White House counsel (he cooperated with congressional investigators and served four months in a federal safe house)*

THE QUEEN OF MEAN

Leona Helmsley, Queen of Mean,
Czarina of Venality,
Gained and lost an empire
In Manhattan hospitality.

She set her sights on Harry,
Gotham real estate tycoon,
Then sent his first wife packing
And devoured him with a spoon.

With the chimes a distant echo
From the Helmsley wedding bells,
Leona wheedled Harry
Into funding swank hotels.

She terrorized her minions
From her flagship Helmsley Palace,
A crass and brassy paragon
Of tyranny and malice.

The fashion plate of kitschy glitz,
She crashed New York society.
Tabloid writers feasted on
Her tawdry notoriety.

But notwithstanding all her wealth
And luxuries galore,
She stuck her fingers in the till
And pilfered millions more.

With addled Harry ruled unfit
In Scottsdale, Arizona,
A charge of dodging income tax
Was leveled at Leona.

A four-year term was handed down.
Community service, too:
Nine hundred hours that sly Leona
Bribed her staff to do.

In the end, she took her leave,
Her swanky brand destroyed.
The social pages lapped it up,
Consumed with schadenfreude.

In death, Leona's disrepute
Continued to increase:
She left twelve million dollars
To her tiny pet Maltese.

Leona Helmsley, Queen of Mean,
The gossipmongers' prey,
We hadn't seen her like again
Until the present day:

A gross Manhattan plutocrat
Whom avarice brought low,
A cheesy boss of real estate,
A tax-evading reprobate,
With jail a fitting final fate,
Like someone else we know.

In the 1970s and '80s, **LEONA HELMSLEY** *ran a chain of luxury hotels in Manhattan with her husband, real estate mogul* **HARRY HELMSLEY**. *When Harry was declared unfit to stand trial, Leona was convicted of tax evasion and mail fraud and jailed for nineteen months. When she died in 2007, she left a twelve-million-dollar trust fund for Trouble, her Maltese dog.*

THE SECRET LIFE OF NEWTS

The shadow of Newt Gingrich falls across our recent history,
An enigma in a riddle in a puzzle in a mystery.
We're baffled by a question, in bemusement and alarm:
How could such a piddling man do such momentous harm?

An eternal adolescent and precocious over-reacher,
Teenage Newt got married to his mathematics teacher.
A busy bee distinguished by his loud, insistent buzz,
He thus began his vain pursuit of who the hell he was.

With his aptitude for calumny, contempt, and dirty tricks,
Newt embraced the notion of a life in politics.
Three times he ran for Congress on the odd semester off
From a gig in western Georgia as a mediocre prof.

Third time lucky, off he went to Washington, DC,
Where he saw the breed of animal that he was meant to be:
An angry monkey in a cage, spoiling for a fight
And hurling his own turds at every Democrat in sight.

When Newt's bare-knuckle activism lifted him to Speaker,
The norms of civil statesmanship were rendered ever weaker.
Bipartisanship was shackled up, with Newt its fiery captor:
Congress at the mercy of a mad velociraptor.

But despite the clout his party would obsequiously hand him,
Their dirty little secret was: not one of them could stand him.
No congressman of recent years is quite so creepy-crawly
(Except for Cruz, McConnell, Nunes, Gohmert, Gaetz, and Hawley).

Newt's downfall was the product of his rabid over-reachment,
Precipitating shutdowns and crusading for impeachment.
He made Clinton's peccadillo a perfidious offense
While secretly indulging in his own concupiscence.

For Newtie was a horndog of the very first degree,
Remembered less for governance than promiscuity.
With a lurid reputation that he carries like a yoke,
The would-be elder statesman is a lame, unfunny joke.

But the joke's on all of us! Observe the Congress Gingrich left us.
His politics of hatred have irreparably cleft us.
A bottom-fed amphibian bred to poison and pollute:
Salamandridae Pleurodelinae, better known as Newt.

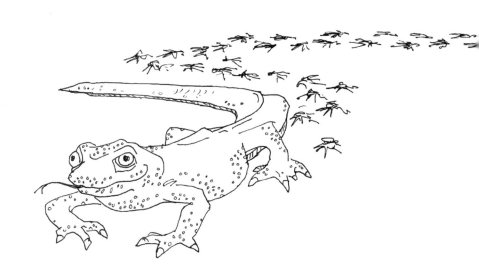

In 1996, **NEWT GINGRICH** *led a shutdown of the government to oppose the policies of* **PRESIDENT BILL CLINTON**. *In 1998, Gingrich led the impeachment of Clinton for perjury related to his extramarital relations with a White House intern. Gingrich himself was simultaneously having an affair with a young congressional staffer. He resigned from Congress the following year.*

MADOFF'S TRADE-OFF

Two thousand eight, that fateful year
When half of us were laid off,
A massive Ponzi scheme collapsed:
The work of Bernie Madoff.

For decades, he had bilked his fund
And gleefully sashayed off,
But then the FBI showed up
And collared Bernie Madoff.

The slackers at the SEC
Had scrupulously stayed off
Since most of them had always been
In bed with Bernie Madoff.

Riches from his faithful flock
Were callously conveyed off
To sate the greed and appetite
Of hungry Bernie Madoff.

Celebrities and charities
Thought every wager paid off.
Affinity fraud was put to use
By pious Bernie Madoff.

Each investor's fiscal skin
Was mercilessly flayed off:
The biggest scam in history
Fattened Bernie Madoff.

His youthful sense of right and wrong
With age had slowly strayed off.
The poster boy of theft is now
Amoral Bernie Madoff.

A widow shamed and two dead sons
Present a gloomy trade-off.
A legacy of disrepute
Has followed Bernie Madoff.

At length, a dreary dirge is heard
As people watch him played off.
They stare with sullen, vacant eyes,
But hardly any of them cries.
Few will mourn a life of lies
Like that of Bernie Madoff.

Financier **BERNARD MADOFF** *amassed nearly sixty-five billion dollars through the biggest Ponzi scheme ever uncovered. In 2009, he was sentenced to 150 years in federal prison, where he died in 2021.*

HAPPY NEW YEAR
A GRAND OLD PARTY, PART TWO

Dumpty funsters, ere you leave,
Share one final New Year's Eve:
2020's almost done,
Likewise all your DC fun.
Four long years flew by too fast.
Power and glory never last.
Celebrate your single term,
All the *drang* and all the *sturm*.
Answer Dumpty's siren call:
Mar-a-Lago's New Year's ball!

Wait a second. This is queer.
Ten to midnight. No one's here.
Where are all the invitees?
Fetch me those RSVPs . . .

Scaramucci missed his flight,
Sekulow mistook the night.
Pruitt's Cadillac broke down.
Dershowitz is out of town.
Someone slashed Jeff Sessions' tire.
Conway set her stove on fire.
Larry Kudlow has a cold.
Wilbur Ross is too damned old.
Bolton stumbled on a stair.
Rudy couldn't fix his hair.
Michael Cohen's still in jail.
No one's heard from Brad Parscale.
Pence, Mnuchin, and Perdue
Thought they might have caught the flu.

Spicer, Price, DeVos, and Barr
Said Palm Beach was just too far.
Bannon, Chao, and Cipollone?
More excuses. All baloney.

But look who made it, just in time,
Each unburdened of his crime,
Free to live a life of ease:
Dumpty's recent pardonees!

Arriving first is Roger Stone,
But he hasn't come alone.
On his heels, Paul Manafort
Slurps a jeroboam of port.
Gliding in is Michael Milken,
His demeanor sly and silken.
Papadopoulos is late
Hefting in a heaping plate
Next to portly Elliott Broidy,
Braying loud and adenoidy.
Charles Kushner enters, flushed with pride,
Dinesh D'Souza by his side,
Joining tipsy Michael Flynn,
Bourbon dribbling down his chin.

Halting chatter tinged with gloom
Echoes in the empty room.
Counting down, they raise a toast
Honoring their absent host.
Flutes of cheap champagne are downed
As the chimes of midnight sound.
Bring on 2021!
Another year has just begun!

Meanwhile, in his private suite,
Dumpty wallows in defeat.
Around him, equally bereft,
The only trusties he has left:
Miller, Hicks, and McEntee
Plus the Dumpty family.
None can manage to cajole him,
Raise his spirits or console him.
Huddled round his slippered feet,
Their desolation is complete.
A distant roar of drunken cheers
Falls on deaf, unheeding ears.
At last, that old familiar line,
The final words of "Auld Lang Syne."

PRESIDENTIAL
SUITE

Members of President Donald Trump's administration included the following:

Vice president
MIKE PENCE

Cabinet
WILLIAM BARR, *attorney general*
ELAINE CHAO, *secretary of transportation*
BETSY DEVOS, *secretary of education*
STEVEN MNUCHIN, *secretary of the Treasury*
GEORGE ERVIN "SONNY" PERDUE, *secretary of agriculture*
TOM PRICE, *secretary of health and human services*
SCOTT PRUITT, *administrator of the Environmental Protection Agency*
WILBUR ROSS, *secretary of commerce*
JEFF SESSIONS, *attorney general*

Advisors
STEVE BANNON, *chief strategist and senior counselor*
JOHN BOLTON, *national security advisor*
KELLYANNE CONWAY, *senior counselor*
HOPE HICKS, *communications director*
LARRY KUDLOW, *director of the National Economic Council*
JARED KUSHNER, *senior advisor*
JOHN MCENTEE, *director of the Presidential Personnel Office*
STEPHEN MILLER, *senior advisor*
BRAD PARSCALE, *2020 campaign manager*
ANTHONY SCARAMUCCI, *communications director*
SEAN SPICER, *press secretary*
IVANKA TRUMP, *senior advisor*

Attorneys
PAT CIPOLLONE
MICHAEL COHEN
ALAN DERSHOWITZ
RUDY GIULIANI
JAY SEKULOW

Pardonees:
ELLIOTT BROIDY, *convicted*
DINESH D'SOUZA, *convicted*
CHARLES KUSHNER, *convicted*
PAUL MANAFORT, *convicted*
MICHAEL MILKEN, *convicted*
GEORGE PAPADOPOULOS, *convicted*
ROGER STONE, *convicted*

MICHAEL FLYNN, *pleaded guilty (twice)*

A ROGUES GALLERY

LIMERICKS FOR THE HERE AND NOW

Until now we have dwelt on the past.
But before we arrive at the last,
Here's a dozen quick takes
About rascals and rakes
From our reprobate present-day cast.

Ted Cruz, that lardaceous baboon,
Is the maestro of inopportune.
With his state in deep freeze
This titan of sleaze
Took his family off to Cancún.

Giuliani, a freak among freaks,
Tends to blunder whenever he speaks.
But his clumsiest mess
Was in front of the press:
Just for Men trickled down both his cheeks.

Marjorie Taylor Greene
Is a fountain of hatred and spleen.
When she opens her trap
Her fanatical crap
Can shatter a video screen.

Joel Greenberg and buddy Matt Gaetz
Share several libidinous traits.
When both of them score,
They tend to ignore
The age of consent of their mates.

The NRA's Wayne LaPierre
Always dressed with extravagant flair.
But he emptied the till
For his toggery bill,
And now he has nothing to wear.

Mike Lindell is the boss of My Pillow
Whose ego continues to billow.
But despite his renown,
His head's full of down,
And he's thick as a sick armadillo.

Alex Jones has a fiendish ability
To monetize rank imbecility.
The best of his tricks
Is to use politics
To sell cures for diminished virility.

Stefanik, in making her mark,
Was as silent and swift as a shark.
She slid in to ensnare
Her conference chair,
While Liz Cheney became Joan of Arc.

Sidney Powell, the POTUS's minion,
Replaced fact with outlandish opinion.
But she trembled with fear
For her tarnished career
When she learned she'd been sued by Dominion.

Ms. Maxwell was Epstein's old flame
Until both were consumed by their shame.
But in all their shared history,
The thorniest mystery
Is how to pronounce her first name.

Republican rube Ron DeSantis
Dreams of ruling a bold New Atlantis.
But with Dumpty behind him,
It's best to remind him
What becomes of the male praying mantis.

Lindsey Graham, that browbeaten fawn,
Is anyone's pliable pawn.
He faces travail
With the balls of a snail
And the spine of a groveling prawn.

Each McConnell political act
Has a physiologic impact.
For Mitch, legislation
Connotes constipation
Of the nation's intestinal tract.

From these verses, you might be inclined
To consider each target maligned.
But compared to their smears
Of the recent few years,
My words have been overly kind.

TED CRUZ, *Texas senator*
RUDY GIULIANI, *Dumpty attorney*
MARJORIE TAYLOR GREENE, *Georgia congresswoman*
JOEL GREENBERG, *former Florida County tax collector*
MATT GAETZ, *Florida congressman*
WAYNE LAPIERRE, *National Rifle Association CEO*
MIKE LINDELL, *My Pillow, Inc., CEO*
ALEX JONES, *InfoWars owner and publisher*
ELISE STEFANIK, *New York congresswoman*
LIZ CHENEY, *Wyoming congresswoman*
SIDNEY POWELL, *Dumpty attorney*
GHISLAINE MAXWELL, *Jeffrey Epstein associate*
JEFFREY EPSTEIN, *convicted sex offender*
RON DESANTIS, *Florida governor*
LINDSEY GRAHAM, *South Carolina senator*
MITCH MCCONNELL, *Kentucky senator*

DUMPTY'S DREAM

At the crack of dawn in Washington, first Wednesday of the year,
The sky was blue, the sun was bright, the air was crystal clear.
Like a child on Christmas morning, Dumpty quivered with excitement
At the prospect of a day of demagogical incitement.

A plot was taking shape that day, transcending all his dramas.
He rehearsed it pacing up and down in slippers and pajamas.
Padding to a window with a view of the Ellipse,
He whispered "Stop the Steal" through a pair of trembling lips.

Elsewhere in the capital, responding to his call,
Thousands of his followers were spoiling for a brawl.
Dumpty's private infantry of goth conventioneers
Had mustered all their forces to secure him four more years.

The night before, they'd gathered for a warm-up demonstration
To stoke the glowing embers for the next day's conflagration.
Their cheers were heard for hours on end throughout the dark metropolis
For pardoned felons Roger Stone, Mike Flynn, and Papadopoulos.

By 8 a.m. they hit the streets, prepared for open battle.
They filled their lungs with frosty air and roared like angry cattle.
Armed with helmets, baseball bats, bear spray, and chest protectors,
They railed against the verdict of the College of Electors.

As Dumpty gave his makeup and his hair a final glance,
His rabble-rousers crowded the Ellipse's broad expanse.
They evoked a mini-Woodstock in a ghastly new edition:
The Summer of Love refashioned as the Winter of Sedition.

They'd assembled there to topple an election they reviled
At a rally Dumpty promised them on Twitter "will be wild!"
The POTUS and his entourage were ushered to a tent
Where he watched with glee the speeches at the start of the event:

Mo Brooks and Amy Kremer and that ravenous akita,
The fierce and fiery Guilfoyle, reenacting her Evita;
Ken Paxton, Donald Junior, and that addle-pated wombat
Rudy Giuliani with his call for "trial by combat."

Drunk on fake conspiracy and manufactured facts,
The hopped-up herd bought every word of Dumpty's opening acts.
Primed for demagoguery and energized by rage,
They howled in adoration when the POTUS took the stage.

What followed was a tirade of interminable duration
With Dumpty spewing cataracts of rank disinformation.
Rehashing all his paranoid and solipsistic themes,
He took boastfulness and grievance to Wagnerian extremes.

The multitude was mirthful when he aimed his brash artillery
At Oprah, Stacey Abrams, Hunter Biden, Joe, and Hillary.
But the raucous celebration turned malignant and unpent
When Dumpty voiced his doubts about his own vice president.

Ten minutes from the rally in an easterly direction,
Congress sat to certify the national election.
Thus Dumpty's words had introduced a note of dark suspense:
The tally would be rendered by Vice President Mike Pence.

Dumpty since November had defied his certain fate,
Hammering officialdom in every crucial state.
By now his only option was to grasp at final straws,
Beseeching Pence to flout the law and put the vote on pause.

The crowd contained a faction of maniacal dissenters:
Oath Keepers, Texas Freedom Force, Proud Boys, and Three Percenters.
As Dumpty's speech meandered, leaving no one unmaligned,
They bolted for the Capitol with murder on their mind.

POTUS finished with a vision of "our brightest days before us,"
And the crowd responded fervently in unironic chorus.
On the heels of the militias, in the grips of Dumpty's thrall,
A many-headed monster lumbered eastward down the Mall.

Post-rally, Dumpty hurried to his White House habitation,
His orange face the picture of postcoital consummation.
He settled in the Oval Office just in time to see
The fruits of all his labors airing live on Fox TV.

In the Capitol, electoral proceedings had begun.
Outside, the western barricades were breached and overrun.
The assembled legislators were completely unaware
As Mike Pence defied the POTUS and ascended to the Chair.

Though the outer doors were guarded by the Capitol police,
They saw their scanty numbers wouldn't long maintain the peace.
They surveyed with ashen faces, surging forth in their direction,
A seething, swelling human sea of angry insurrection.

The horde streamed up the granite steps past every cop and sentry,
Smashing every windowpane to gain illegal entry.
Desperate calls to activate the waiting National Guard
Were greeted by the Pentagon with baffling disregard.

Once inside, the raging tide continued to advance,
Shaking the Rotunda with their caterwauling chants.
The senators and congressmen, in panic and confusion,
Were hustled from their chambers and sequestered in seclusion.

Ramping up the anarchy with cries of jubilation,
The rioters ran roughshod through the temple of the nation.
Capitol security, so grievously outmanned,
Fought in vain through stress and pain to make a final stand.

At the White House, Dumpty reveled in this mutinous typhoon
Like a happy toddler bingeing on his favorite cartoon.
Throwing fuel upon the fire, he sent out a peevish tweet
Attacking Pence's willingness to certify defeat.

The effect on the protesters was ferocious and galvanic,
Their chants of "Hang Mike Pence!" becoming murderous and manic.
The dogs of war were baying, bloody chaos was let loose,
And high above the rabble rose a scaffold and a noose.

The invasion, like a torrent wiping out a DC picnic,
Swept away a Capitol policeman, Brian Sicknick,
Then claimed a second victim at the Speaker's Lobby door:
Ashli Babbitt took a bullet and fell backward to the floor.

Minority chief McCarthy, in his desperate hour of need,
Got Dumpty on the phone and begged his boss to intercede.
Though Kevin was by habit Dumpty's deferential drudge,
Despite his frantic plea, the sodden POTUS wouldn't budge.

Lounging in the Oval, Dumpty sipped a Diet Coke
And with slack self-satisfaction cracked a condescending joke:
"Well, Kev," he said, and wiped a blob of ketchup off his shoe,
"It looks like this election has them more upset than you."

With the melee grabbing half the planet's horrified attention,
Dumpty's inner circle staged a nervous intervention.
They timidly suggested that the POTUS might release
A presidential order to stand down and keep the peace.

Dumpty grudgingly consented in a sour and surly sulk.
He polished off his Burger King and hoisted up his bulk,
Then stood before a camera and addressed the angry mob,
Concealing his delight at how they'd carried out their job.

In its paper-thin hypocrisy, his video epistle
Was a minute-long rendition of his usual dog whistle.
Between the lines, he signaled "voter fraud" with wordless clarity
And offered up "We love you" with transparent insincerity.

But Dumpty's words, alas, were far too little and too late.
The damage was inflicted, and the horse had left the gate.
On the Hill, the mob receded, their destructive passion spent,
Convinced that they'd exulted their exalted president.

The Capitol lay desecrated, vandalized, and scarred
At the tragic late arrival of the luckless National Guard.
They beheld the bludgeoned victims of the brutalizing throng,
Soldiers in a war against a monumental wrong.

At 8 p.m., like hostages delivered from a cage,
Congress reassembled in a state of righteous rage.
After hiding out for hours in political perdition,
They were stubbornly intent upon accomplishing their mission.

Straining on past midnight, they ignored the passing hours,
Their heavy lift a peaceful shift of governmental powers.
Across the floor at 10 to 4, at last the vote was called:
Joe Biden, a new president, was finally installed.

At dawn, the Congress stumbled out past stacks of trash and rubble,
Riding out a day and night of terror, toil, and trouble.
Though haunted by the echo of the long-departed crowd,
Our beleaguered old democracy was bloodied but unbowed.

In the White House, Dumpty thundered after thirty sleepless hours,
Raging at the loss of all his autocratic powers.
But his fury sputtered unexpressed for lack of a transmitter:
His ravings had been muted by his banishment from Twitter.

He staggered to his bedroom where he crumpled in a heap.
His adrenaline expended, he was desperate for sleep.
His head, beset by tortured thoughts, was pounding like a drum,
But when soothing sleep descended, Dumpty dreamed of things to come.

He dreamed that Democrats would pass Impeachment Number Two
For inciting insurrection and a plotted palace coup;
That a handful of Republicans would fearlessly stand by them,
But that Dumpty, once acquitted, would completely crucify them;

That McCarthy, who'd exhibited a modicum of spine,
Would travel down to truckle at the Mar-a-Lago shrine;
That McConnell, after slamming Dumpty on the Senate floor,
Said he'd absolutely vote for him in 2024.

POTUS dreamed he'd be an absentee at Joe's inauguration,
The fourth of only four throughout the history of the nation.
Despite his courtroom belly flops, he dreamed he wouldn't quit
Since Joe's administration wouldn't ever be legit.

He dreamed that he'd fall silent in his tenure's aftermath,
Lying low at Mar-a-Lago to devise his future path.
With a keynote speech at CPAC, he'd regain his strident voice
And prove that he remained his party's overwhelming choice.

He dreamed of three combative years, a struggle for survival,
Stirring anger, stoking fears, and smashing every rival.
He dreamed that in the end he would ascend to seventh heaven:
He'd win the White House once again, as *POTUS 47!*

Take a breath and contemplate the sixth of January,
A traumatizing memory impossible to bury;
A wound that left us reeling from a feral public breach,
The catastrophic consequence of one despotic speech.

A sunny dream for Dumpty is a nightmare for the rest of us.
The health of our democracy demands the very best of us.
For years our body politic was beaten black and blue:
The cure is making sure that Dumpty's dream does not come true.

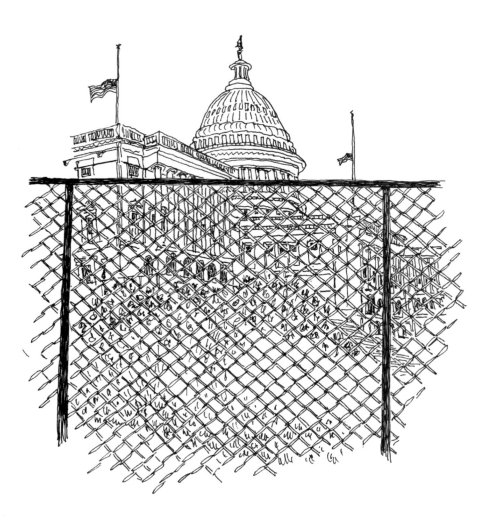

RICHARD M. NIXON

RUDY GIULIANI

WILLIAM M. TWEED

SARAH HOWE

ALEX JONES

WILLIAM P. BARR

JOHN N. MITCHELL

ATCHISON

ALBERT B. FALL

MATT GAETZ

THEODORE BILBO

LINDSEY GRAHAM

J. R. BRINKLEY

ROY M. COHN

RON DE SANTIS

MARJORIE TAYLOR GREENE

CUSTER

WAYNE LAPIERRE

SPIRO T. AGNEW

SIDNEY POWELL

ELISE STEFANIK

ANDREW JACKSON

MICHAEL T. FLYNN

BERNARD MADOFF

NEWT GINGRICH

LEONA HELMSLEY

FORREST

TED CRUZ

MITCH MCCONNELL

MIKE LINDELL

MARY MALLON

TILLMAN